GHB Guide
(Gamma hydroxybutyrate)

*A Definitive Guide and Safety Information,
Technical Details and GHB Spec.*

TABLE OF CONTENT

INTRODUCTION

Along with MDMA, gamma hydroxybutyrate, often known as GHB, has earned a reputation as a "party drug," even though it is associated with several significant hazards.

To present you with the most accurate and objective information that is possible, we will examine GHB from a subjective point of view in this book. A great deal of information, including the effects, the typical dosage, the potential dangers of using it, and more, will be included.

CHAPTER ONE

What is GHB?

Gamma hydroxybutyrate, often known as GHB ($C_4H_8O_3$), is a depressant that acts on the central nervous system (CNS). It is frequently known as a "club drug" or a "date rape" drug on account of its reputation. Teenagers and young adults are known to misuse GHB in a variety of settings, including bars, parties, clubs, and "raves" (all-night dance parties). Additionally, GHB is frequently found in alcoholic beverages. Individuals who misuse GHB have reported experiencing beneficial benefits such as euphoria, enhanced sex desire, and calm. A number of adverse effects, including but not limited to sweating, loss of consciousness, nausea, hallucinations, forgetfulness, and coma, may be experienced by the individual.

In 2002, the Food and Drug Administration (FDA) granted approval for the brand-name prescription medication Xyrem (sodium oxybate) for the treatment of narcolepsy, a sleep disorder that is characterized by excessive drowsiness and recurrent episodes of daytime sleepiness. The sodium salt of gamma hydroxybutyrate is one of its components. In the United States, Xyrem is a medicine that is subject to stringent regulations. Because it is a prohibited drug that falls under Schedule III, patients are required to engage in a restricted access program.

Another naturally occurring metabolite of the inhibitory neurotransmitter gamma-aminobutyric acid (GABA) that is present in the brain is called gamma-hydroxybutyrate (GHB). The amounts of the naturally occurring metabolite GHB that are detected in the brain are far lower than the levels that are typically seen in the brain when the substance is misused. Some beers and wines may contain trace amounts of natural GHB as a consequence of fermentation, although these amounts are not large enough to be considered detectable.

GHB Specs & Technical Details

Chemical Name	Gamma-hydroxybutyrate
Street Names	G, Grievous Bodily Harm, Fantasy, Liquid Ecstasy, Liquid X, Liquid E, Soap, Blue Nitro,

	Fishies, Juice, Georgia Home Boy, Cherry Meth, Scoop, Goop, Gina, Georgia, Easy Lay, Geeb, Sleep-500
Duration of Effects	1-2 hours
Level of Risk	Medium-High

What's The Dose of GHB?

It has been stated that the most typical dosage range for GHB is between 0.5 and 1.5 milliliters.

Both of these doses are quite low. An overdose might be caused by a difference of only one milliliter of fluids. This medicine is extremely hazardous for several reasons, and this is one of them. When a person is already inebriated, it is quite simple for them to make an incorrect estimation of the dosage, which might lead to severe repercussions.

Because greater doses might create undesirable side effects such as blackouts, nausea, and other complications, the majority of users stick to or stay below the 1 mL level.

GHB (Gomma-Hydroxybulyrole)

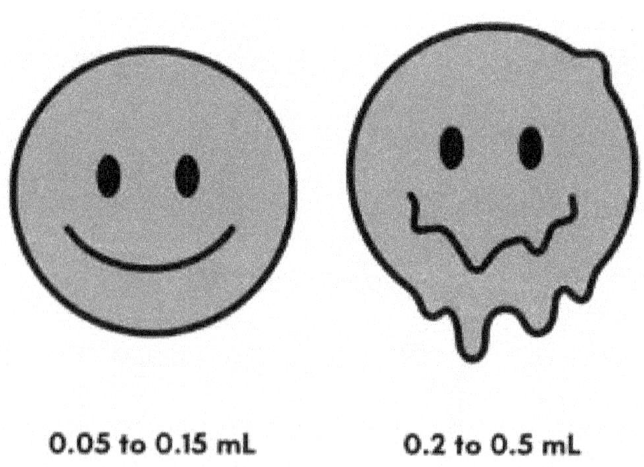

0.05 to 0.15 mL   0.2 to 0.5 mL

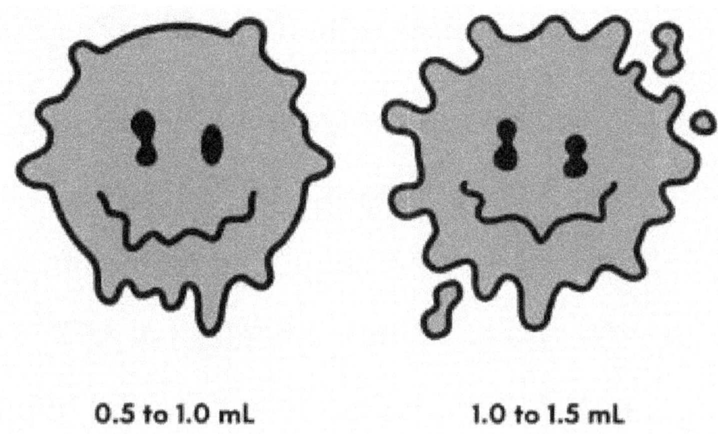

0.5 to 1.0 mL
1.0 to 1.5 mL

Can You Microdose GHB?

The technique of administering sub-perceptual dosages of psychoactive chemicals is referred to as microdosing at this point. When people use LSD or magic mushrooms, this is a typical habit that they engage in.

In a technical sense, it is possible to microdose anything, even GHB, by simply consuming extremely small dosages of the substance (usually around 10 percent of a standard dose). According to this, a microdose of GHB is somewhere between 0.05 and 0.15 milliliters.

Taking relatively modest amounts of GHB, according to the claims of some individuals, may boost creative output, sociability, and introspection. Some people believe that the GABAergic effects are responsible for their increased sense of peace and relaxation.

CHAPTER TWO

What Does GHB Feel Like?

When people talk about GHB, they typically refer to it as a "combination of MDMA and alcohol." Users have a sensation of pleasure and vitality that cannot be denied, in addition to the fact that they feel inebriated and frequently begin to lose muscular coordination similar to that of alcohol.

Not only is there a correlation between GHB and an increased libido, but it is also associated with auditory or visual hallucinations (at larger dosages), as well as a feeling of calm and contentment.

Blackouts are a common side effect of taking excessive amounts of GHB. People who use this substance wake up the next morning with very little to no recollection of the previous night.

Does GHB Cause a Hangover?

Many assert that GHB does not result in a hangover. Even though the symptoms that occur the following day are not the same as those that occur after a heavy night of drinking (headache, nausea, lethargy, and dizziness), GHB displays a distinct hangover pattern in individuals who consume moderate to high dosages of the substance.

GHB hangovers are more comparable to MDMA than they are to any other substance. This condition is characterized by a "dull" experience in which users are unable to concentrate and are unable to think of the appropriate phrases to utilize. A great number of users have reported feeling uninspired, sluggish, or inanimate.

Although the precise etiology of the hangover is unknown, probably, the effects of the drug on the central nervous system (CNS) might result in a temporary dependence on the substance. A change in the amounts of acetylcholine, serotonin, and dopamine in the brain is known to occur when GHB is present.

After the effects of GHB have worn off, the majority of users who do have hangover symptoms do not notice them until twelve to twenty-four hours later. Some people who utilize it over an extended period may experience prolonged hangover symptoms.

How Long Does GHB Last?

Approximately twenty to sixty minutes after ingesting GHB, the effects of the substance reach their height. In the majority of cases, the effects continue for around two to three hours before disappearing entirely.

The bulk of the substance is metabolized and eliminated from the body over a period of twelve hours, but GHB can stay in the bloodstream for up to about twenty-four hours. The vast majority of drug tests are unable to identify GHB; however, specialized tests have the ability to detect the chemical for up to forty-eight hours.

CHAPTER THREE

GHB Strength vs. Other Psychoactive Compounds?

Even though GHB is a psychedelic drug that is relatively potent, it does not induce the same distortion of reality that you might anticipate from substances such as LSD, DMT, or mushrooms such as mushrooms. The psychedelic experience that the majority of people refer to as being associated with these substances, which involves both auditory and visual hallucinations, is less powerful while using GHB.

When compared to MDMA, GHB is a more accurate comparison because the tremendous euphoria that it produces is often the impact that people seek out the most. When compared to the euphoria that they experience from MDMA, some users believe that the euphoria that they experience from GHB is more powerful and more gratifying.

On the other hand, if the medication is used often, tolerance to GHB can develop quite rapidly. For users to have the same degree of effects, they need to take progressively greater doses. In certain cases, this might result in an individual overdosing, which can have disastrous consequences, such as unconsciousness, hostility, risky conduct, and even death.

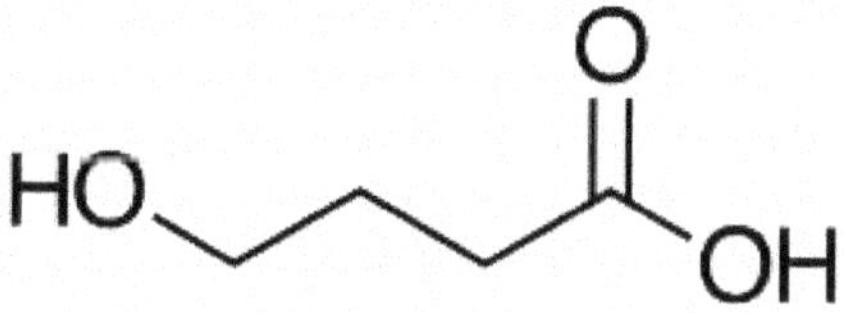

GHB

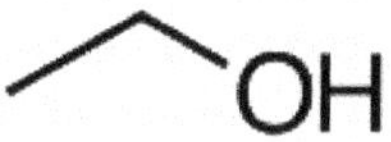

Ethanol

GHB vs. Alcohol

It is common practice to consider GHB to be an alternative to alcohol. It results in a state of intoxication somewhat comparable to that of alcohol, as well as greater sociability and lower inhibition.

On the other hand, GHB is substantially more calming than alcohol, particularly when used in smaller amounts, and the pleasure that it produces is significantly stronger.

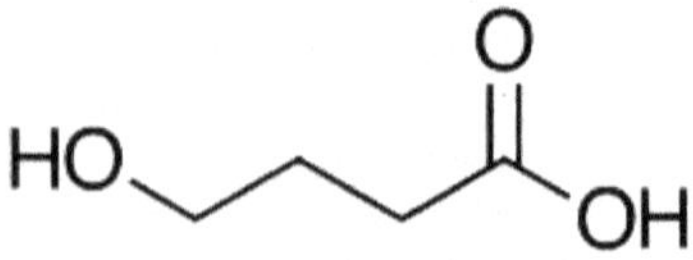

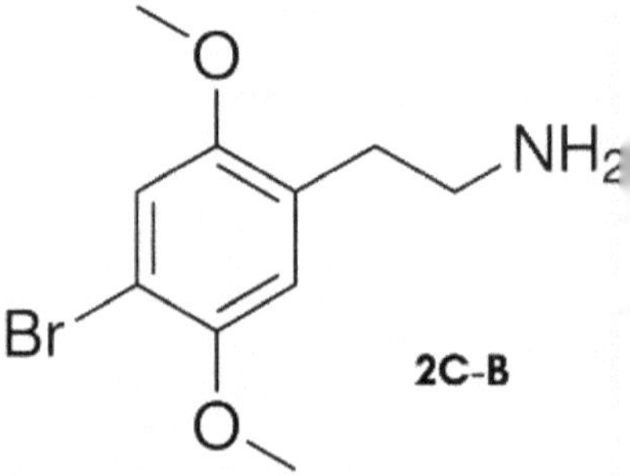

Unfortunately, it is far simpler to overdose on GHB than it is on alcohol, even though the consequences, which include blackout, memory loss, and erratic behavior, are comparable.

GHB vs. 2C-B

2C-B is a medication that belongs to the wider family of pharmaceuticals known as 2C-X. Every single one of the 2Cs is based on mescaline, which is a naturally occurring hallucinogenic that may be found in peyote cactus or San Pedro cacti.

In some ways, the effects of 2C-B, 2C-I, 2C-E, and other members of this group are comparable to those of GHB; nonetheless, there are significant distinctions between the two.

Both GHB and 2C-B are referred regarded as "party drugs" due to their capacity to promote feelings of pleasure and sociability while simultaneously lowering inhibitions. This, however, is where the similarities come to a stop. The effects of 2C-B are significantly more euphoric, psychedelic, and long-lasting than those of 2C-B. The experiences are quite distinct from one another.

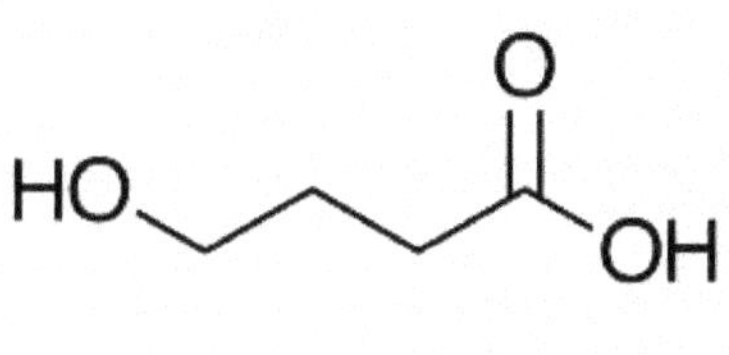

GHB

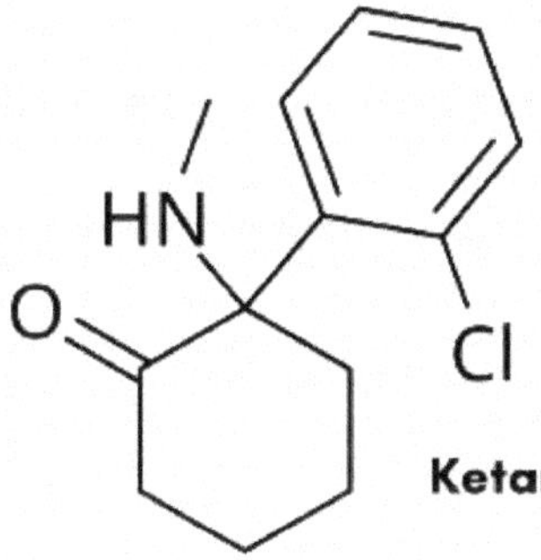

Ketamine

GHB vs. Ketamine

PCP and MXE are both examples of medications that belong to the arylcyclohexylamine class, which is also the class that ketamine belongs to.

As is the case with GHB, ketamine is frequently used as a party drug. At lesser dosages, it is analogous to MDMA in that it produces a state of dissociation that is equivalent to that of alcohol or GHB, and it brings about an enhancement in the vividness of colors and lights.

However, the processes by which these medications exert their effects are quite different. Ketamine is more "trippier" than GHB, and it does not have as big of an impact on sociability or connection with other people. It tends to induce individuals to turn more within, experiencing the lights and noises of their environment from within, rather than deriving the way they feel based on the energy of the people around them.

CHAPTER FOUR

Is GHB Safe?

As is the case with any substance, GHB has the potential to be unsafe and even lethal if it is overused or misused.

A significant number of fatalities have been documented with time, and hospitalizations following the consumption of this chemical are not unusual.

Although it is possible to use this medication without experiencing any long-term adverse effects, it is of the utmost importance to be aware of the dosage that you are taking and to avoid combining it with other substances or alcohol.

GHB is a highly powerful substance. Depending on the dilution, the effects can result in major negative effects if even one milliliter is taken in excess, or if it is mixed with other substances that depress the central nervous system, such as alcohol.

To achieve the intended consequences of intoxication, blood concentrations of 80–100 mg/L are required, however, concentrations as low as 300–500 mg/L might result in mortality.

Respiratory depression, often known as inefficient breathing, and circulatory collapse are known to be the most prevalent causes of mortality resulting from an overdose of GHB (widespread destruction of blood cells and tissue or cardiac arrest).

Typical Signs of GHB Overdose

GHB overdose occurs in a short amount of time. After around twenty minutes of consumption, this chemical that is rapidly absorbed begins to exert its effects, and by sixty minutes, it has reached its maximum levels.

A common misunderstanding is that the symptoms of a GHB overdose are the same as those of alcohol consumption, which may be lethal. To prevent respiratory depression or cardiac arrest from occurring, emergency care must be delivered as fast as possible.

An extremely low heart rate, dizziness or fainting, and a major alteration in awareness are the primary indicators that should raise your concern when dealing with someone you feel is overdosing on GHB (unable to answer simple questions about who they are, where they are, or what day it is). It is estimated that around fifty percent of cases of GHB overdose involve vomiting.

What are the symptoms of a GHB overdose?

- Hallucinations
- Slurred speech

- Nausea & vomiting
- Miosis (constricted pupils)
- Bruxism (jaw grinding)
- Hypothermia (reduced body temperature)
- Ataxia (uncoordinated movements)
- Amnesia (sudden memory loss)
- Tremors
- Disorientation & confusion
- Bradycardia (slow heart rate)
- Hypotension (low blood pressure)
- Delusions
- Altered or absent breathing
- Gaze nystagmus (involuntary eye movement; up and down or left & right)

GHB Adulteration

The manufacturing and selling of GHB on the black market are not subject to any regulations because it is illegal. Although it is available for purchase as a prescription medication known as Xyrem, which is meant to treat narcolepsy, the sale of GHB or Xyrem for recreational use immediately places it in the Schedule I category of drugs.

When you ingest GHB, you probably won't always be aware of what you're putting into your body because there is no regulation for the substance. The unlawful production of this substance frequently involves the combination of GBL (gamma-butyrolactone) with hazardous compounds that are found in drain cleaning or lye. Consuming these compounds may be extremely hazardous, and in some cases even fatal.

GHB Drug Interactions

Because GHB is a somewhat powerful depressive that acts on the central nervous system, mixing it with any other depressant, including alcohol, can be highly risky. GHB must never be combined with any other narcotics, even though it is frequently used as a party drug. One of the most prevalent reasons for an overdose of GHB is doing anything that is against this guideline.

Short-term effects of GHB

In most cases, the effects of GHB are experienced within fifteen minutes and continue for around three to four hours. Depending on the amount of GHB that is consumed, the effects might vary substantially. For example, lesser doses of GHB can be more stimulating, while bigger amounts can be more sedative.

The effects of a substance can be significantly amplified by a very minor increase in its quantity. When it comes to the use of GHB, this is one of the most hazardous features. There is a very slight distinction between the quantity that a person may ingest to have the intended effect and the amount that will cause them to overdose on the substance.

Always begin with a modest dosage and wait until you feel the effects before further.

Among the effects of GHB are the following:

- Tremors
- Tunnel vision
- Hallucinations
- Relaxation
- Drowsiness

- Sociability

- Euphoria

- Vomiting

- Blackouts and memory lapses

- Seizures

- Coma

- Respiratory arrest (stopping breathing) and death.

- Lack of inhibition

- Increased sex drive

- Loss of coordination (ataxia)

- Confusion, irritation, and agitation

- Heightened sensitivity to touch dizziness

GHB – Dependence, Tolerance, And Withdrawal

There are three types of reliance on GHB: psychological, physical, or both. In a short amount of time, tolerance and reliance can develop in those who take GHB regularly. On the other hand, this indicates that people wish to take ever-greater amounts in an effort to attain the same impact. On the other hand, this may potentially result in an intensification of the undesirable side effects.

You may have withdrawal symptoms if you are reliant on GHB and you suddenly stop taking it. This is because your body will need to readjust to operate correctly without GHB.

If you wish to quit taking GHB, you should first consult with a qualified medical practitioner. Withdrawal symptoms can be extremely severe and even possibly fatal. It is typical for them to begin around twelve hours after the previous dose and can endure for approximately fifteen days.

A sudden withdrawal from large dosages may result in severe

symptoms, which may necessitate the aid of a certified medical professional.

Long-Term Effects Of GHB Use

There is a lack of information on the effects of GHB over a longer period of time; yet, it is known that the substance can lead to dependency.

Other long-term impacts that have been observed include:

- Heart disease
- Hallucinations
- Severe memory problems
- Extreme anxiety
- Breathing problems.

GHB Use in Pregnancy

When it comes to human pregnancy, the effects of GHB usage remain unknown. The use of GHB by pregnant women is strongly discouraged. Women who are pregnant or who are considering becoming pregnant and who use GHB should seek the counsel of a healthcare practitioner as soon as possible.

CHAPTER FIVE

Does GHB induce addiction?

GHB indeed has the potential to be addictive. The levels of several neurotransmitters in the brain, including serotonin, dopamine, and GABA, are altered as a result of the medication application. Substances that alter the chemical composition of the brain have the potential to become addictive. The majority of people who use GHB do so seldom that they do not develop a dependence on the substance; nonetheless, continuous usage can swiftly lead to addiction being developed.

It is possible for withdrawal from GHB to be exceedingly difficult, and it can occasionally result in seizures, despair, and even physical death. Becoming dependent on GHB is something that should be treated extremely seriously and should be avoided at all costs.

Depending on the degree of dependence, the first indications of GHB withdrawal often occur around twenty-four hours after the last time the substance was used. These symptoms can continue anywhere from twenty-four hours to seven days.

Symptoms of withdrawal from GHB:

- Insomnia

- Sweating

- Tachycardia

- Tremors

- Vomiting

- Abdominal cramps

- Anxiety

- Diarrhea

- Seizures (rare)

- Hypertension

- Nausea

- Restlessness

- Hallucinations & delusions (rare)

- Rhabdomyolysis (rare).

Legality of GHB

In the United States, GHB has been classified as a Schedule I drug since the year 2000, and in the European Union, it has been classified as such since the year 2001. This classification indicates that the sale, possession, and use of this substance are all tightly forbidden.

Xyrem is a type of GHB that is only available with a doctor's prescription and is used to treat narcolepsy. It is permissible to use Xyrem when it is administered by a qualified medical professional. A felony offense is deemed to be the act of selling Xyrem.

How Does GHB Work?

In the majority of cases, GHB is responsible for inhibiting the activity of the GABA receptors, which are located in the central nervous system.

This is a method of action that is utilized by both alcohol and benzodiazepines, with the exception of a very small distinction. When it comes to hypnotics, ethanol and benzodiazepines are effective on the GABA A subtype, but GHB is effective on the GABA B subtype. GABA A has an impact that is more rapid but only lasts for a short period, whereas GABA B has an inhibitory effect that is slower but lasts for a longer time.

An analogy may be made between GABA and the brake pedal of the neurological system. Glutamate and other neurotransmitters that are stimulating can be reversed by this substance, which serves to slow down nerve transmission and counteract the stimulating effects of others. Additional GABAergic substances, such as benzodiazepines, are utilized to decrease the activity of the nervous system in order to either alleviate anxiety or make it easier to fall asleep.

Another potential cause of intoxication is the agonistic action of the GABA receptors. Therefore, the actions of GHB on GABA are responsible for its capacity to create sensations of relaxation (in low doses), enhanced sociability and intoxication (in moderate doses), and anesthesia (in high doses) (in higher doses).

Last but not least, GHB has the ability to stimulate the activation of GABA receptors in the brain, which can result in a state of relaxation and drowsiness.

Is It Dangerous?

Yes, there are a lot of ways in which GHB is hazardous.

Given that GHB is illegal, there are no regulations in place to regulate the potency and purity of the medications that are manufactured. Drugs that are offered under the name GHB frequently contain unknown substances or other fillers, some of which may be hazardous. Both the amount of GHB that is present in the solution and the safe dose are unknown to you.

When using GHB, it is simple to take an excessive amount, to overdose. There have been reports of fatalities. When used with alcohol or other drugs, the effects of GHB are amplified, and the danger of experiencing toxic consequences and overdosing is increased. Other substances, such as alcohol, are typically involved in fatalities that are caused by GHB.

The use of GHB, which is a powerful sedative, causes users to lose consciousness and enter a deep slumber from which they may not awaken for several hours. During the night, they could throw up and suffocate on their vomit. Convulsions and difficulty breathing are two symptoms that may be experienced by those who are in a GHB sleep. Sometimes, when users wake up, they find out that their friends or family members have brought them to the hospital for immediate medical attention.

The liquid form of GHB makes it possible to conceal it in beverages, and the sleepy effects of the substance prevent victims from putting up a fight against sexual assault. In addition, GHB has the potential to induce amnesia, which means that once individuals have recovered from the effects of the drug, they cannot recall what took place.

Certain drugs, such as protease inhibitors, which are used to treat HIV, have the potential to combine destructively with GHB.

Because sleep may come on rapidly after taking GHB, driving after taking this substance is exceedingly risky. Drivers and operators of machinery who are under the influence of GHB or any other substance are at an increased risk of sustaining bodily injuries, not just for themselves but also for others around them.

Methods of GHB Abuse

It is possible to obtain GHB in the form of an odorless and colorless substance, which may be mixed with alcohol and administered to victims who are unaware of the risks involved before sexual attacks. The flavor might be described as salty or soapy. As a result of its use for sexual assault, GHB has earned the reputation of being a "date rape" material. As a result of the sedative effects of GHB, victims become unable to resist sexual assault since they regain their ability to function normally. It is also possible for GHB to cause amnesia in its victim. High school and college students, as well as people who attend rave parties, are common users of GHB because of the exhilarating effects it produces upon use.

It is also hypothesized that GHB has anabolic benefits since it stimulates the production of proteins. Bodybuilders have utilized GHB to increase their muscle mass and decrease their body fat percentage.

The illegal substance known as GHB may be purchased in liquid or powdered form, either on the street or over the Internet. It is used for illegal purposes.

Consumption of it is done through the mouth, and it is usually mixed with alcohol. There is a significant amount of GHB that is created in clandestine labs and may be found on the streets or the internet. GHB may have been tampered with with unknown impurities, which might make it much more hazardous. To produce GHB, it is customarily necessary to combine lye or drain cleaner with GBL, which is a chemical relative of GHB and an industrial solvent that is frequently utilized to perform floor stripping.

The advice was published by the Food and Drug Administration (FDA) in 1990, stating that the use of GHB was harmful and unlawful, except for procedures that were approved by the FDA and monitored by a physician. Under the Controlled Substances Act, GHB was classified as a Schedule I substance in March of the year 2000.

When it is given to a patient and used lawfully under a patient-restricted-access program, the sodium salt of GHB, which is sold under the trade name Xyrem (sodium oxybate), is categorized as a Schedule III substance by the Drug Enforcement Administration (DEA). It is not possible to purchase Xyrem at conventional retail pharmacies. If Xyrem is sold for recreational purposes, its status will change to Schedule I, which means that it will be considered an illegal narcotic.

Frequently Asked Questions About GHB

The questions that are included here are some of the most frequently asked inquiries concerning GHB.

1. Can a Single Use of GHB Lead to Addiction?

Even after a single dose, there is little evidence to suggest that GHB possesses the ability to build habits or become addicted. The majority of persons who use GHB do so in a moderate manner.

It is conceivable for someone to become obsessed with the effects of GHB and feel a compulsive need to use it again, despite the fact that it is extremely unusual for someone to become physically addicted to GHB after only one session of using it without any prior experience.

Some individuals have a higher propensity than others to develop an addiction to drugs that affect their state of mind. The likelihood of an individual being addicted to GHB or other narcotics can be affected by a variety of factors, including their individual physiology, mental health state, and cultural influences.

2. Is GHB Dangerous?

The distinctions between a recreational dosage and a dose that can be fatal are so minute that GHB can be highly hazardous because these variances are so small. Additionally, the risk of GHB is significantly increased when it is used with other sedatives or hypnotics, in addition to alcohol. As a result of the environment in which this drug is most frequently taken (at clubs, pubs, or parties), there is a great probability that an individual may mix GHB with other narcotics without being aware of the repercussions of doing so.

3. When Was GHB Invented?

The prodrug of GHB, known as GBL (γ-butyrolactone), was initially developed by the scientist Alexander Saytzeff in the year 1874 in the country of Russia.

Before the late 1960s, when Dr. Henri Laborit started looking at it in greater depth, there was a period of about one hundred years during which nothing occurred. GHB and GABA, which are the principal neuroinhibitors in the brain, were found to have structures that were comparable to one another. He was of the opinion that GHB had the potential to raise the levels of GABA in the brain, which would be beneficial in the treatment of a variety of psychiatric problems, including anxiety, sleeplessness, and other illnesses.

4. Is GHB Formed During Ketosis?

The body can't manufacture GHB on its own. On the other hand, it is an isomer of β-hydroxybutyrate (BHB), which is one of the principal ketones that the body produces when it is in a state of famine. It acts as a substitute for glucose as a source of fuel in situations where glucose levels are low.

During the 1980s and 1990s, GHB was utilized by dieters and bodybuilders alike due to the widespread belief that it facilitated the reduction of fat. With its parallels to BHB, which at the time was not well known, it is possible that this impact was caused by its similarities.

In the interest of full disclosure, GHB has never been demonstrated to be effective in promoting fat metabolism or weight reduction.

There is still a lack of clarity on the possible impact that GHB and BHB might have on brain function as a consequence of ketosis.

CONCLUSION

When compared to alcohol and MDMA, gamma-hydroxybutyrate, often known as GHB, is most frequently examined. At regular dosages, it offers a degree of relaxation that is comparable to that of alcohol, but it also produces a body high that is far more powerful. In addition, it causes a pleasure that is somewhat less severe than the bliss that you would experience from ecstasy, but it also provides a significant increase in sexual desire and sociability.

When used in excessive amounts, GHB may be extremely hazardous and even lethal. It also has the potential to cause users to develop an addiction to the substance and experience unpleasant withdrawal symptoms if it is used too frequently.

When you decide to use GHB, the most important thing to keep in mind is to make sure that you are completely certain about the dosage and to avoid mixing it with any other substances, especially substances that are classified as CBS depressants, such as alcohol, phenibut, or benzodiazepines.